Rob's story is one that can be very beneficial to young couples as they follow God's plan. The "Eight Financial Principles" from the Bible have been taught by individuals in our firm for over 40 years. May this book be a road map to success and significance in family stewardship to many.

- Derek Lewis, President
J. Derek Lewis & Associates

Robby's story and perspective is refreshing. His book engages the reader and provides a clear biblical view of stewardship and integrates principles of wise financial management. I highly recommend this book for any reader who wants to grow in their stewardship journey.

- Doug Hyepock, Investment Adviser, CFP®, ChFC
J. Derek Lewis & Associates

Steward From The Start

Robert W. Knutsen

ISBN:1717436684
ISBN-13:9781717436689

DEDICATION

I consider myself the richest man because God has
blessed me with four of His prized possessions. My wife
Holly, my boys Brady and Brock, and my princess Sadie! I
cherish each one of you deeply and I thank God for
choosing me to be his steward as a husband and father.

CONTENTS

ACKNOWLEDGMENTS

I am the result of the many people who have invested in me: family, friends, co-workers, teachers, pastors and mentors. I appreciate each of you deeply.

A special thank you is owed to Derek and Nancy Lewis for the countless hours they have spent mentoring, encouraging, supporting and loving me. They have consistently modeled so many of the stewardship principles mentioned in this book and remind me always to give credit to He who is worthy, our Lord and Savior Jesus Christ.

Thank you to the team at J. Derek Lewis & Associates for the wisdom shared over the years. Each one of you has played a vital role in my life and I am blessed to be surrounded by such wonderful people.

Thank you Bruce Anderson for your guidance and expertise in taking this book from an idea to a work that I believe will help many families. Working with you was a blessing.

1 THE BEGINNING

A bicycle is one of a ten year-old boy's most prized possessions. One Christmas, I had my heart set on a very specific bike. I began hinting, nudging, begging and praying -- out loud, right next to my parents -- for months leading up to Christmas. I actually posted pictures of the bike all over the house and set the family computer background and screensaver to an image of the bike. I knew it was over the dollar amount my parents typically spend for Christmas, but hoped it was close enough.

Christmas finally came, and my two older brothers received their big gifts. I had a handful of smaller gifts, but nothing was left under the tree. My first thought was that my parents were punishing me for relentlessly begging them. I sat there, probably pouting, while they cleaned up the gift wrap and moved on to breakfast. What I didn't notice was my dad slipping out and then riding up to the door on The Bike.

I took meticulous care of that bicycle and spent many years enjoying it. Eventually, I outgrew the bike, and it didn't see much action. A young guy at our church needed a way to get to and from school, so I saw this as a great opportunity to bless him. He lit up as I handed this beautiful machine over to him, and I felt great about it.

Two weeks later, I saw him riding up to church. As he approached, I thought he must be riding a different bike. It had been sloppily spray-painted silver and was almost unrecognizable.

Arriving, he jumped off and let it hit the ground with a crash. My beautiful bike had been trashed in a few days! The cheerful giver in me flipped upside down, and I regretted my decision.

As I re-lived that memory, I couldn't help but think of the many things God has given me that I have squandered. **Stewardship is defined as the careful and responsible**

management of something entrusted to one's care. Although this book will primarily focus on financial stewardship, the Bible goes far beyond our finances. Biblical stewardship refers to the use of God-given resources (time, talent, treasure, truth, relationships, etc.) for the accomplishment of God-given goals. Keep that in mind when you think about your own and your children's activities.

It's never too early or too late to put these principles into practice. If we don't learn about handling money and teach our children, the whole family can expect to learn the hard way.

But it doesn't have to be like that.

2 THE PROMISE

Michael Jackson was a billion-dollar pop singer who sold more than 60 million records around the world. Yet he died $400 million in debt. Why? Every year, he spent more than he made.

Isn't that an obvious outcome?

At J. Derek Lewis & Associates, we have had some very difficult conversations with people who are forced to make tough financial decisions because of their actions in the past. Like gravity, money can be cruel.

Most of these individuals didn't intentionally dig themselves into a financial hole. They ended up there because of what they didn't know. A few were aware that their financial life was not sustainable and chose to stay on that course anyway. But more often, we meet people with savings, retirement accounts and insurance, yet they don't know what they have, why they have it, if it will be "enough," or whether they should be doing more.

Countless studies show that informed consumers are considerably more likely to purchase a product than people who don't understand how or why that product might help them. The same concept can be applied to financial literacy. The majority of Americans haven't taken the proper steps towards their retirement, not because they aren't aware of its importance, but because they feel the concepts are overwhelming and out of reach.

Take a look at these eye-opening facts:

- Nearly 6 in 10 Americans don't have enough savings to cover a $1,000 unplanned expense [1]
- More than half of workers have less than $25,000 in savings and investments that could be used for retirement, not counting their primary residence or defined benefits plans such as traditional pensions [2]

- Arguing about money ranks first among predictors of divorce (3)
- The Bible has roughly 2,350 passages on money and how to give, save and spend it wisely. In contrast, the Bible has some 500 verses about prayer and roughly 500 verses about faith. Our stewardship is one of the great tests of our spirituality. (4)

We hope this book will move you from the unknown to the known, and allow you to help those over whom you have influence to do so as well. Our goal is to enrich life, making every life we touch better as a result. We accomplish that by guiding people in their stewardship.

This book is designed to help parents and grandparents recognize and implement basic stewardship principles in their own life, and then model and teach them to those whom they influence at each stage of life.

I have yet to find someone who has not made a bad financial decision. Far from trying to make you feel bad about your financial past, this book was written with an eye toward the future. It will either be a reminder to you or it may expose you to new ideas. It will equip you with the ability to raise stewards from the start.

Your earthly reward will be financial peace, through a full dependence on God, and the blessing of responsible children who will in turn be good stewards over God's resources. Many of these principles, if acted on, have the potential to eliminate conflict over money with your children.

The eternal reward is hearing, "Well done, good and faithful servant; you were faithful over a few things, I will make you ruler over many things. Enter into the joy of your lord." (Matthew 25:21)

Are you ready to get started?

3 LIFELONG FOUNDATIONS

Imagine yourself the parent in a family of five, taking a vacation across the country that includes an airliner, rental car, hotels and many other details. It sounds like a lot of fun, and everyone is looking forward to it.

Did I mention that your three children are ages five and under?

No parent would embark on that type of adventure without a tremendous amount of planning. It may begin months ahead of time, and the final weeks would be filled with packing and prepping for all anticipated disasters. A well-thought-out plan can result in a fairly pleasant experience at the airport, a flight with plenty of activities and snacks, and an arrival at the hotel just as the sugar crashes hit and meltdowns begin. *Planning makes all the difference.*

The sad reality, however, is that many families spend more time organizing a vacation than they do their finances. Granted, the vacation reward is more immediate and tangible, but the consequences of neglecting financial plans are much more severe … and life-changing.

To get started on our journey toward financial health, let me share a few principles that will be like signposts to help guide the way. Keep these in mind as you go through the rest of the book.

Acknowledge that God owns it all. This is the foundation principle of good stewardship. We must first acknowledge whose resources we are managing. According to the Bible, "The earth is the Lord's, and everything in it, the world, and all who live in it" (Psalm 24:1).

Many people, myself included, are captivated by "if only" thoughts. If only I had a certain balance in my checking account. If only I made more money. If only I get that car, promotion, dream job, vacation home, boat, bike, clothing … and the list goes on and on.

Although we would probably deny it, we secretly tend to believe that money and/or things can provide us peace. "If I had a couple of million dollars, I wouldn't have to worry anymore." However, God is the only one who can give peace. Money and possessions can all be gone in the blink of an eye, no matter how much you have. Be thankful for what God has entrusted to you, and be sure to manage and use it well.

Spend less than you make. Create a budget and stay within it, or you will quickly lose track of where you are. For some, that is accomplished by actually putting cash into envelopes each designated for a specific purpose. Others may create a budget ahead of time, giving each dollar a name to ensure they spend less than they make. This allows a margin so you can save for unforeseen circumstances. It also provides an opportunity to respond when you feel that God is calling you to give. Many websites and apps can help you with a budget.

Avoid debt whenever possible. The Bible has much to say about this. For example, "The rich rule over the poor, and the borrower is slave to the lender" (Proverbs 22:7 NIV) and "Let no debt remain outstanding, except the continuing debt to love one another" (Romans 13:8 NIV). Debt has the ability to rob us of our freedom. Stop paying for the past so you can start planning for the future!

Believe it or not, earlier generations actually saved up for a large purchase such as a car. Banks offered Christmas savings clubs where you could regularly put money away, at interest, in order to pay for presents at the time you bought them. Families lived in smaller houses – and were happy – rather than take on a huge mortgage. Although this seems like common sense, it certainly isn't common practice today.

Give generously. It is not hard to find stories of people who have buckets of money, yet are still unhappy. There are few things more satisfying than the ability to help someone else achieve a dream they had little chance of accomplishing on their own. When asking God how to best use our resources, WE can be the answer to someone else's prayer. Giving is a key part of stewardship, because it requires us to trust God and helps keep us from becoming selfish.

Think long-term. Fear is one of the most crippling emotions. Steady plodding brings prosperity, yet many times we allow the fear caused by short-term events to destroy our long-term plans. The majority of individual stock market investors earn less than the market average because fear causes them to pull out at the wrong time. As the legendary mutual fund manager Peter Lynch put it, "Far more money has been lost by investors preparing for market corrections, or trying to anticipate corrections, than has been lost in the corrections themselves."

It's important to have perspective. In the summer of 2017, there was great excitement when a total eclipse of the sun was visible across much of the United States. It is incredible that the moon is able to completely block the sun from Earth's view, given the fact that the sun is so large (it could hold 64 million moons inside).

Quite often, investors fixate on events that are relatively small, like the moon, and ignore things that in comparison are massive and vital to our very existence. Some focus on the daily volatility of the stock market. Many fret over the exaggerated 24/7 media cycle. The long-term view, however, assumes that these things will average out over time, and does not give in to fear.

Build reserves. It is wise to save a portion of your earnings for future expenses, which allows you to avoid debt and also exercise discipline. This is an example of what economists call Opportunity Cost, which refers to a benefit that a person could have received, but has given up in order to take another course of action. Stated another way, an opportunity cost represents the alternative you lost when a decision was made.

For example, an avid coffee drinker could easily spend $5 per day at Starbucks. Let's say you gave up the coffee and decided to invest that money instead, adding up to about $150 per month. Assuming your investments averaged 10 percent annual rate of return, you could have $113,404 in 20 years. If you are able to stick with it for 40 years, you could have $876,333.

On the other hand, forty years' worth of coffee would cost you $72,000. So the opportunity cost of a $5 cup of coffee per day, for 40 years, would be $804,333. This thought may have ruined the taste of coffee for you, or you might say, "I love my coffee, and I am not willing to give it up." The important point is that nearly everyone could find a way to save $5 per day and reap a huge reward over time.

Don't go it alone. The Bible says, "In an abundance of counselors there is victory" (Proverbs 24:6 NASB). An adviser can be there to help you see all sides of the decisions you make and help you determine the right one. In addition, accountability helps ensure discipline. A successful financial steward does not travel alone, but leans on professionals with expertise in areas where the person is not comfortable. Collaboration allows for new and fresh ideas to help you reach your goals and objectives.

Geese provide a great example of working together. As each goose flaps its wings, it creates an uplift for the birds that follow. By flying in a "V" formation, the whole flock adds 70 percent to its flying range. At the same time, the geese honk to encourage those up front to keep up their speed. It is a silly illustration, but a great parallel to our stewardship journeys. We need to travel with others who will encourage us and support us along the way.

Share your successes and failures. Superman was the first big comic book superhero, yet Batman is far more popular. Why the difference? Batman is flawed and has character. Superman is too perfect. He is practically invulnerable and can also fly.

Too often we try to present our financial situation as if we were invincible, even to our families. We bury our flaws and failures, portray ourselves positively on social media and never let our guard down. Yet our kids and others are looking for someone believable to connect with.

There is much to be learned from people who have been there or done that. Share your successes, and also share your failures in the hope that others can avoid the same mistakes. This honesty principle is key for parents and grandparents to guide their children. How many times do we struggle with something and think, "Had I only known…"? Vulnerability can radically change relationships and take them to a whole new level. Just be you!

So in conclusion, what do all of these principles have in common? The recurring themes are planning, self-discipline, long-term thinking and concern for others. Now, with these values in mind, let's begin finding out how to manage, model and teach good financial stewardship at each stage of life.

(For a list of eight money principles from the Bible, see the end of this book.)

4 LIFE STAGE – BIRTH TO KINDERGARTEN

As a parent, were you ever horrified to see your child do or say something that was just like you? I recently heard my two-year-old tell her older brothers to "knock it off or you are going to your room." That must be something that I say often, and yes, she does believe that she has that authority.

The early years are the most impressionable, and it's never too soon to think about what kind of model you are for children or grandchildren. What ideas are you helping to mold, and what kind of legacy are you leaving behind?

This also applies to finances. The principles absorbed by preschool and kindergarten children will last a lifetime. As the Bible says, in an often-quoted verse, "Train a child in the way he should go, and when he is old he will not turn from it" (Proverbs 22:6).

At this stage of life, the lessons are more caught than taught. To young children, food, clothes and toys may seem to magically appear, and few kids would connect them to the parent going off to work in the morning. How often do they actually see real cash changing hands when you pay for something significant, as opposed to a credit card or a few taps on a smartphone?

The most important foundation is what the parent thinks about the source of finances, along with everything else necessary for life. **Who is ultimately responsible for the family's income?** As quoted in the last chapter, "The earth is the Lord's, and everything in it, the world, and all who live in it" (Psalm 24:1).

Do you remember to give thanks to God for his blessings, and encourage your children to join in? Is he acknowledged as the source of all good things? Do you point out what has been entrusted to your care, and the importance of managing it well?

Just as a parent is responsible to God, he or she is also responsible to the family, and this should be modeled and taught. Every major decision has an impact on your spouse and children, even if it seems primarily to be a personal decision. For example, you may be considering a new job. It may require you to travel and be away from home more, but also pays better than your last job. Flip that scenario around and think about a change that would pay less but allow you to spend more time with your kids. Which road do you take?

Marriage itself involves stewardship responsibilities, as well as a tremendous amount of care and attention. The effects of divorce certainly weigh on the entire family, and like many stewardship decisions, can have multi-generational effects. Be sure to have the conversations, teach your children about the daily choices you make for your family, and then reinforce the responsibility God has placed upon you by entrusting them to your care. I always tell myself, "As a father, every one of my decisions is a generational decision. My choices will have an impact on my wife and children."

A key ingredient in stewardship is a **solid work ethic** to handle our responsibilities.

This is something you can teach as well as model. Encourage little ones to complete tasks and do everything to the best of their ability. Instead of simply buying children something outright, provide them with an opportunity to earn at least some of the money needed to make the purchase. This will display the tangible benefit of working, and experiences such as this will reinforce the relationship between time and money, effort and reward.

A variation on this is the concept of **delayed gratification**. It has been said that raising financially disciplined children in an undisciplined society may be the hardest task parents face today. Generally, delayed gratification is associated with resisting a smaller but more immediate reward in order to receive a larger or more enduring reward later.

How can this be taught in a society where you can simply speak to "Alexa" and Amazon Prime is ready to deliver? One example of teaching this principle is having children contribute to a savings account for future desires they may have, such as a toy or special party dress. This can be as simple as a piggy bank or a special jar on a high shelf. In addition to giving kids the experience of being able to acquire something they really want by saving – and waiting – for it, this system also reinforces the concept of limited resources. When the money is gone, you cannot buy something you might like to have, no matter how much you really want it.

In support of this savings idea, some families give a regular allowance even to young children. It can be a regular gift from the parents or earnings from simple chores, such as cleaning up the room or helping with the dishes. Or it can be both. Whatever the source, an allowance helps children learn – with guidance and encouragement -- how to divide their resources between what can be spent now and what needs to be saved for a larger reward later.

Just as important is the concept of **giving to others**. Again, modeling is crucial. Be a generous family, and bring children into the conversation when appropriate. Let them know why your family is giving to the church, charity, family member, friend, etc. Encourage them to set some of their money aside for giving, and help them with opportunities.

Keep a special jar or bank on the dinner table to which the whole family can contribute. At Christmas, adopt a needy family in your area, and involve the children in buying and making a holiday meal. Sponsor an orphan. Have the children give to the church out of their own funds instead of handing them money on Sunday morning.

Whatever methods you find appropriate for your family, it's important to model and teach the meaning of finances from an early age. The children will be spared the stress and worry of financial problems, and you will avoid having them come to you in desperation later in life!

5 LIFE STAGE – ELEMENTARY SCHOOL

Pizza Day! That was Friday when I was in elementary school. I can still picture getting that brown cardboard tray with a thick slice of Ball Park pizza and a small carton of chocolate milk. That is, assuming I still had one of the five dollars my mom gave me on Mondays. If I overspent that week, come Friday I was packing a lunch and watching others enjoy Pizza Day.

Elementary school is the stage of life where children can begin to really understand what money is and the value of managing it. A weekly income helps children experience financial stewardship and teaches many key life lessons. Parents should allow their kids to make some mistakes along the way with their money, while the consequences are small, ensuring that they learn the right lessons from them.

Here are a few thoughts on **children's allowances**:

- The amount will vary from family to family, but you should consider things such as age, maturity level, need, and the family's financial situation
- Review the amount periodically on some determined schedule, such as the start of the school year, calendar year, birthdays, etc.
- Set expectations, but give the kids freedom to make mistakes
- Set up accountability meetings to review spending and talk about the decisions they made
- Teach them to plan and budget their money, then review how they did
- Be sure to guide them into giving and saving as part of what they do with allowance money
- Remember that your kids are watching. Make sure to model the principles you are trying to teach them.

An important goal in giving allowances is to help kids understand the concept of **limited**

resources. Until a child learns to prioritize needs and wants, he won't be able to make the hard choices that life is sure to send his way

At this age, children can also learn to **compare prices**. This is the beginning of understanding what things actually cost, what the alternatives are, and how to make a decision based on this understanding. The quality of a product might justify a premium cost, but evaluating your options gives you the ability to make an informed decision.

It's also helpful to involve your children in **family finance meetings**. Sit down together in an informal setting and discuss the financial decisions you are making. Talk about the cost of groceries and household items the children probably take for granted.

Equally important, discuss money that the family will be giving to others. **Tithing** regularly at church acknowledges that it is God's money and you are a steward over it. A tithe is an act of trusting that God will provide. If your children aren't already giving at church, now is the time to begin. The Bible says in Malachi 3:10, "Bring the whole tithe into the storehouse, that there may be food in my house. Test me in this, says the LORD Almighty, and see if I will not throw open the floodgates of heaven and pour out so much blessing that there will not be room enough to store it."

This life stage is a great opportunity to lay the foundation. Your children may not fully comprehend the lessons being taught, but they are listening, watching and learning. Keep reinforcing these foundational principles and be intentional by regularly bringing them up and highlighting real-life examples as they occur. Let your actions speak so loudly that they don't even need to hear what you're saying.

6 LIFE STAGE – HIGH SCHOOL

A family with two teenaged girls had been using an allowance system that provided their children with money every week. In the summer, they added a school clothing allowance. One particular year, the kids were given $250 for school clothes. The first girl went to a discount retailer and was able to buy five new outfits. The other spent the entire amount on one outfit from a high-end store.

The first day of school was awesome, but a high school girl could never be caught wearing the same clothes two days in a row. She soon realized she had made a mistake, and started selling other belongings to buy more clothes. This turned out to be a great teachable moment.

High school is a great time to start **transitioning an allowance to an income**. It is certainly a family decision whether you want your kids to work outside of the house while going to school and juggling extracurricular activities. However, this is a crucial time where they can experience the challenge of earning money, paying taxes, meeting expenses and saving for emergencies. It's quite an eye-opener when they discover how little of a paycheck is left after tax withholding, Social Security, etc.

Once a young person starts earning an income, he or she should begin learning the details of **investing and saving** for the future. If you have a financial adviser, the kids should meet with him to help understand the importance of investing and catch a long-term vision. I personally was fortunate to have had such an opportunity as a young man. I truly appreciated my parent's wisdom and guidance, but as a high schooler, I was much more receptive to others' influence.

The greatest component to any investment plan is time. The earlier people start, the more they can experience the **power of compounding**, whereby the earnings of an account multiply. Over long periods of time, this can make a significant difference.

Take the example of two co-workers —
Jim and Joe. They saved the same amount of
money in their firm's retirement plan ($300 a
month for 30 years for a total of $108,000) and
earned the same annual return (8%). The only
difference is that Jim began investing at age
25, and Joe waited until he was 35. The bottom
line: By age 65 Jim had accumulated $912,330
while Joe's balance was $422,585. That's a
significant advantage for Jim, thanks to getting
an early start.

Another way to think of compound
interest is *"interest on interest."* It means the
interest you earn each year is added to your
principal, so the balance doesn't merely grow,
it grows at an increasing rate. Albert Einstein
called it "the greatest mathematical discovery
of all time." Compound interest is an investor's
best friend and also a borrower's worst enemy.

In Chapter 3, we talked about
opportunity cost, which refers to a benefit
that a person could have received but gave up
to take another course of action. We used the
example of giving up a $5 daily expense for
coffee.

Along with relative prices of what a

teenager can buy, almost every purchase we make is an example of opportunity cost. You can buy a pair of jeans for $20 or $200. Is the quality of the $200 pair ten times the quality of the $20 pair? Would one good pair outlast ten cheap pairs? The opportunity cost in this example is dependent on some variables, but still makes a significant difference. High school is the time for young people to learn about this.

A major decision for most students and their families during the high school years is **how to pay for college**. Hopefully, the family has been thinking about this for some time and saving for it. College tuition is often a mix of family savings, student earnings during the school year and/or summer, and loans.

A few years ago I met a young man who was three days away from his freshman year at a private Christian university. It also happened to be my alma mater and a place where I had had an incredible experience. His brother asked that I speak to him as a graduate and provide some financial perspective.

The first question I asked was, "Why did you choose this particular college?" He said his siblings went there and they had seemed to like it, but it wasn't really where he wanted to go. My next question was, "How are you going to pay for it?" He replied that he had met with an admissions counselor, and they set him up with some student loans. The amount was roughly $115,000 for four years.

I followed up by asking if he knew how he would repay a loan that size. He responded like any other 18-year-old would, assuming that he would be making enough money after graduation to cover the cost. What he didn't realize was that six months to the day after graduation, he would be on the hook for $1,500 per month. If he wanted to move out of his parents' house, drive a car, have a social life and pay $1,500 a month on student debt, he would need a pretty significant income out of the gate.

The problem with debt is that it has control over your decisions. Student debt of that magnitude would certainly limit what he is able to do after he finishes school. He finally decided that he wasn't comfortable borrowing that amount of money, now that he understood it fully. He decided to attend junior college to take care of his undergraduate classes, until he really was sure what he wanted to do. Even if he chooses to graduate from that private university, two years at a junior college will save him nearly $60,000.

It is vital that students know what they are getting into when they take on student loans. Even if the family is going to pay for their college education, they should still understand the sacrifice made for them. Like any loan, it is best not to learn about the details from the interested party. The admissions department will lay out the details and help you determine what kind of aid you qualify for, but they are also doing everything they can to reach full enrollment. In most cases, they are not going to explain what borrowing funds of that magnitude will mean in the form of repayment. They will likely highlight the increased earning potential of a college degree -- and that is true -- just not the whole picture.

Some of the college tuition problems we see with our clients include:

- Parents neglecting to save for retirement in order to pay for their kids' school
- Parents pulling funds from their retirement savings to send their kids to school
- Students borrowing without understanding the payback details

- Students spending a lot of money pursuing one interest, only to realize they would prefer to do something else.

Our advice to parents is to first make sure they are managing their own retirement plans before paying for college. Students have the ability to earn or sensibly borrow their way through school, and can find cost-effective ways to attend college.

One of the top concerns we experience with retirees is a fear of becoming a financial burden to their kids. This can happen by neglecting or liquidating retirement savings to fund a college education. The Apostle Paul wrote, "I will not be a burden to you, because what I want is not your possessions but you. After all, children should not have to save up for their parents, but parents for their children" (2 Cor. 12:14).

The key to sensibly borrowing funds for college is understanding the details. Before students agree to a loan, they should know the true cost and exactly what the payments will look like. We have seen many graduates give up their freedom upon graduation because of the income required to service their debt. The ability to take a year or two off after school to travel or serve on a missions trip may not be an option if you have a large monthly student loan payment.

We also see students extend their time in school because their interests have changed. If you graduate from high school and don't have clue what you want to do, think about going to a junior college to take care of some undergraduate core classes and save money while you decide.

High school is also a great age to have significant **family finance meetings**, which hopefully began in elementary school (Chapter 5). Using a parent's discretion about sharing information, this is a great way to open students' eyes to the real world. Show them the cost of the basics: food, clothing, utilities, housing, etc. Knowing what things cost will help them realize what is in store for them as adults, and it will also create some buy-in at home. They may be more careful with the items you provide them, or take better care of the assets you own.

You can also share with them your financial wins and losses. Talk about your giving, retirement planning, budget, vacation cost and anything that can help them understand the why behind your stewardship decisions.

A married couple can show teenagers how you work together to reach your financial goals. For example, you might always consult your spouse before spending a certain dollar amount. Money has a tremendous effect on relationships, and teaching children to have healthy conversations about it while the stakes are small is vital.

At this age many young people have some sort of an income. In addition to tithing on allowances, which can be taught very early in life, the sooner you can model, teach and encourage **tithing** on earned money, the easier it will be. Tithing acknowledges that God owns it and that we trust him to provide. Giving is one of the most rewarding parts of my life, and I have yet to meet someone who wished they would have been less generous. If one waits until they have enough money to give, it is more than likely they will never begin.

7 LIFE STAGE - COLLEGE

College, in the context of stewardship, should be treated as an extremely valuable resource. It is a privilege to attend college in the first place. Only a third of American adults have a four-year college degree, and that is the highest level ever recorded. (5)

Many young adults attend college hoping to discover what they are passionate about, and end up spending extra time in school and more money as they change their minds and switch majors. Another group of students sees it as a ticket to freedom, and they party their way through school, doing just enough to earn a diploma. Others invest the time and energy extracting as much as they possibly can out of their time in college. They get involved, study, build relationships, get to know their professors and make the most out of the experience.

Most college students want to be treated as adults, with maximum personal freedom, and colleges generally take this view as well. However, these young people are in most cases dependent upon others for support, generate little or no discretionary income and have few responsibilities other than earning good grades. Does the phrase "have your cake and eat it too" fit here?

This might be the last time a parent or grandparent can have significant influence on the choices and direction of a young person for whom they are responsible, so it's important to make every lesson count.

After college will come a career, so these years provide a perfect opportunity to get some experience and **try a number of different jobs**. An internship is a great way for a young person to see whether a particular field is of interest or not. Some know what they want to do and find an internship that confirms their desire. It sometimes turns into a job offer, or is at least a great addition to their resume. Others discover that the reality of a particular job doesn't match the dream. Regardless, an internship allows a person to try something, when the stakes are low, and see if it's worth all the effort and education.

Many college professors spent time in the field prior to joining academia. Building a relationship with your professors not only enables you to get the most out of the course, but they often have connections in that particular field than can lead to interviews and internships. I personally still get together with a handful of my professors to seek their wisdom and guidance.

Because college students usually have control over how their personal money is spent, whatever the source, these years should certainly involve a **budget**, which is simply a spending plan. No one would build a house without a plan, knowing details of each cost associated with the project. You wouldn't be sure if it was possible to build the house without knowing what it might cost.

Most people would agree that spending less than you make is the key to avoiding debt and financial freedom. A plan helps you to do just that. If the source of the student's funds is a parent or grandparent, it can certainly come with strings attached. Ask for a budget proposal, or review spending with the student at the end of each month. This can be a great teaching opportunity, and provide accountability while the stakes are still low.

The student should start each month by allocating every dollar he or she will earn or withdraw from an account. That will ensure staying on track. If something unexpected comes along, the student can reduce spending in another category, tap into an emergency fund, or at least know that the month was overspent and has to be made up. There are many great spending trackers available today. Whether using a smartphone app, updating a spreadsheet, or tracking spending by hand, find what works and get started. As the famous writer Antoine de Saint-Exupéry said, *"A goal without a plan is just a wish."*

Credit card companies are delighted to offer a card to college students, in the hope that they will have a customer for life. Signing up for one can be a convenience or a disaster. It tempts one to make impulse purchases regardless of whether or not the funds are available to pay for them. For some people, a low-limit credit card might be a good way to find out how much self-discipline they have.

Having credit and beginning monthly payments is a life-changing event, and is often one of the factors that move the focus of our lives from where it should be. "The rich rule over the poor, and the borrower is servant to the lender" (Prov. 22:7). A general rule of thumb is to avoid debt if at all possible, and try not to borrow in order to buy a depreciating item (which is most everything except a house or an education!).

We talked in the last chapter about **student loans**. They can be a good investment if borrowed sensibly. The bottom line is that a college degree does improve the odds of stable employment and a higher salary, but it is no guarantee. The only guarantee is that you will have to pay back what you borrow, and with interest. By recognizing the value of a college education and taking advantage of all of the opportunities that the environment offers, a college graduate will confidently know it was a good investment. But even if the time is spent well, it is still important to find the most sensible way to fund one's education. See Chapter 6 for more thoughts on student loans.

If you have followed the recommendations in previous chapters, you have taught your children and grandchildren the importance of **tithing**. College age is where this discipline tends to be lost, because college students have very little income and are on a tight budget, with a lot of opportunity to spend. Yet what better time to practice the principle in Luke 16:10-12: "Whoever can be trusted with very little can also be trusted with much, and whoever is dishonest with very little will also be dishonest with much. So if you have not been trustworthy in handling worldly wealth, who will trust you with true riches? And if you have not been trustworthy with someone else's property, who will give you property of your own?"

This is a time for young people to exercise sound stewardship over all of their gifts. The opportunity to go to college is extremely valuable. They should make the most of it, through hard work, and remember where this blessing has come from. According to Olympic champion Jesse Owens, "We all have dreams. But in order to make dreams into reality, it takes an awful lot of determination, dedication, self-discipline, and effort."

8 LIFE STAGE - CAREER

At the wise old age of 21, I sat excitedly with my graduating class. I remember being unable to listen to the wisdom that was shared in the various commencement speeches because my diploma had already been earned. I was just a few steps and a handshake away from being a college graduate, confident that my education and the diploma would be my ticket to a wildly successful career. Fortunately, I already had full-time employment lined up, thanks to a successful internship. Yet I still needed to perform, and that sometimes involves learning from mistakes.

The transition from college to career is significant because our mistakes and failures shift from a botched exam or presentation to real-life rewards and consequences. Reggie Jackson is known for his impressive baseball career, and is even called Mr. October for his clutch hitting, yet he also leads the league in career strikeouts, with nearly 2,600. He was not afraid to step up to the plate over and over again and swing. Mistakes should not be devastating, but instead be a motivation to do better next time.

While this book is primarily about helping children and grandchildren understand financial stewardship, it's important to take stock of where your own family – or your children's families – is as well. It's amazing how many mature people neglect the basics when it comes to planning.

One often-overlooked factor is the need to have **insurance**. Some Christians view insurance as a failure to trust the Lord, but from a stewardship perspective, not having insurance shows a lack of consideration for the family. While there are many different types of insurance and reasons for them, the core for a family with children is **life insurance**.

If something were to happen to mom or dad, would the family be OK from a financial standpoint? Until there are enough savings to replace the loss of income, term life insurance is the way to go. It allows you to cost-effectively protect your family from such a catastrophic event. Eventually, the term of coverage will expire, and with proper planning, by then you would have enough savings and reduced liabilities to take care of your family. Insurance needs can differ greatly, so be sure to buy only what you need, not necessarily what the sales person suggests.

Closely related to having insurance is **writing a will** and naming guardians for your children. Whom would you want caring for them in the event of a catastrophe? If you don't have a will, the state will decide, after potentially putting them first into a group home or foster care. They will typically look at blood line, but I would safely bet this is a decision you want to make for yourself. Drafting a will is a simple process, and you can modify it as circumstances change over time.

In addition, you should consider creating a **living trust**. This is a legal entity that actually owns your stuff. You place your assets into the trust, and then you or an appointed person serves as trustee, to hold, manage, utilize and ultimately distribute to your designated beneficiaries. A revocable living trust is very flexible, and is designed to be adjusted as circumstances change.

The alternative is **probate** after your death. Nobody enjoys the probate process. Simply stated, probate is a systematic, court-supervised process where a deceased person's estate is evaluated and administered. Debts and taxes are settled, court mandated fees are paid to attorneys and, ultimately, your loved ones receive what is left.

If you live in California, it can take roughly a year to settle and distribute an estate. Probate is not determined by having a will or not; it has everything to do with ownership. If you own a home or assets worth $150,000 or more, your estate will go through probate. The cost is determined by the fair market value of the estate's property. Hypothetically, an estate with a $700,000 house, plus savings and investments valued at $800,000, could pay roughly $58,000 in probate fees in addition to a painful, lengthy process. So the nominal cost of establishing a living trust pales in comparison to the cost of probate.

An equally important financial safeguard is having an **emergency fund**, which can be difficult if you are barely making ends meet. A general rule of thumb is to be able to cover 3-6 months of your income. That can serve to support you if you were to lose your job, and give you some time to find a new one. It can also be used to handle an unforeseen expense without causing you to take on debt. Many people rely on their credit cards as their emergency fund, and it is often "emergencies" that start the snowballing of debt that traps them into an endless cycle of poverty.

During this stage of life, you are likely to be making some **significant purchases**, such as a house or cars. As discussed in previous chapters, consider saving up some or all of the purchase price before buying. This is probably impractical in the case of a house, so carefully consider the type of mortgage loan you are taking.

Some consider **mortgages** to be a good type of debt. Unlike a car, a house is hopefully going to increase in market value over time. If you sell it years down the line, you may net enough of a profit to offset some of the principal and interest you've paid on the loan. Home loans also tend to carry lower interest rates than personal loans, and the interest you pay is tax-deductible, adding to your overall savings. The key with a mortgage is to borrow within your means and avoid overextending yourself. Be aware that in the early years you are paying mostly interest, so plan to stay in your house a while if you are taking out a mortgage.

By now, **tithing** has hopefully become a fundamental part of your finances. If not, this is the time to begin. For many, the career stage is the first time they are earning a substantial income. It may seem challenging to tithe now, because the amount you write on a weekly check can be substantial. But the Lord says, "Test me in this" (Malachi 3:10). It can take a significant amount of faith, but this is one of the ways we can demonstrate that we trust the Lord and put him first. God calls us to build his Kingdom with the money he has entrusted to us. The Bible instructs, "Each of you should give what you have decided in your heart to give, not reluctantly or under compulsion, for God loves a cheerful giver" (2 Corinthians 9:7).

Tithing should be part of your **budgeting**, which is crucial for getting through the career stage successfully. One doesn't just drift into the desires of their heart. Oliver Wendell Holmes said, "To reach a port we must sail, sometimes with the wind and sometimes against it. But we must not drift or lie at anchor." Without proper budgeting, you will likely end up in an undesirable financial position. When you do create a plan, stick with it, check your progress and be accountable to someone. You will have a much greater chance of making it there.

Most people struggle with saving, setting goals, planning and budgeting for four main reasons:

1) They are unaware. They don't know exactly what is at stake when they ignore these foundational principles.

2) They are preoccupied. They might be stuck chasing a promotion or are consumed by their current wants, with the thought that they will start saving once they reach a particular milestone.

3) They are busy. Sometimes people become so distracted by daily life that they leave no margin for things that are really important.

4) They are misled. Whether it is the culture's spending habits, slick marketing campaigns, self-justification, herd mentality or lack of a financial role model, people often rationalize their way out of sound financial management.

As a result, according to the federal Bureau of Economic Analysis, Americans on average save less than 5% of their disposable income. From 1950 to 2000, it was twice that (often with just one spouse working!). Experts believe that a 10-15% savings rate is required to accumulate an adequate retirement nest egg.

Here are some ideas to help you save:

- **Automate your saving**. When you have a job, the government collects taxes from every paycheck. This method is far less painful than paying a lump sum monthly or annually. You can use a similar approach for saving. Ask your employer or payroll service to set up an automatic withdrawal from each paycheck. This removes the money before it goes into your checking account. If your employer doesn't provide this option, use an automatic bank transfer from checking to savings. The goal is to move the money out of an account that you use for paying bills or routine spending.
- **Pay yourself**. Another saving method is to write your savings account a regular check, as if it were a creditor. The idea

is that you actually owe money to yourself and must pay your account like any other debt. (If you don't write checks, transfer money from your regular account to a savings account.) It's best to put this into a Money Market account that earns interest, as it remains unused.

- **Use the savings snowball**. When an existing debt, such as a car loan, is paid off, reallocate the money that was going toward that debt to your savings account. This will allow you to snowball the amount allocated to savings as you steadily pay off debts.

An important incentive to saving is a good understanding of **compound interest**, as was mentioned in Chapter 6. This phenomenon, which is basically the interest earned on interest, has the potential to radically change your life – for better or for worse. Compound interest has historically allowed those who earn it to realize their financial goals and dreams, yet dramatically hinder those who pay it. The good news is that you get to determine whether it will be your best friend or worst enemy.

For example, if you put $2,000 into a 3%

savings account, you earn $60 in the first year and end up with $2060. Assuming you leave the interest in there, the next year you earn $61.80 (the 3% on your original investment plus 3% on the $60 earned the previous year).

On the other hand, if you have a $2,000 debt at 10% interest, you will be charged $200 (2000 x 0.10) after the first year. The debt is now $2,200. The second year, you are again charged 10% interest, which this time comes out to $220 (2200 x 0.10), so now you have $2,420 of debt. You can see how it begins to add up quickly!

Along with financial planning comes **family planning**, which can have a dramatic impact on the success of your family. There are definitely some stewardship principles to consider. Time is the first that comes to mind. Do you have the margin to manage your time in a way that your spouse and children will require? That will take sacrifices in other areas of your life. The second is finances. Are you in a position to take on the financial responsibility of bringing a child into the world? The third is the responsibility of raising a family in the way of the Lord. This is incredibly important to God and a tremendous stewardship responsibility.

Tied in with all of these is the concept of **legacy planning**, to make sure that your life unfolds in a way that reflects your principles and goals. This is far more about preserving your values than it is about money. Creating a financial legacy plan will help clarify your family's shared purposes; it should not be left to chance. Once you are crystal clear on these, you can easily communicate them to the next generation. Perpetuating wealth across many generations requires leading a diverse group of people -- your heirs -- to align around your vision, values and legacy plan. Good planning will help them avoid being part of the statistic that 70% of family money is usually gone by the end of the second generation and 90% by the end of the third generation.

Some keys to legacy planning include:

- Identifying what inspires you
- Creating giving goals
- Engaging the next generation
- Working with an advisor to maximize your giving potential. There are many tax-advantaged ways to give, and a proper strategy can drastically increase your giving potential.
- Considering a foundation account or a donor advised account (see Chapter

10). Either of these can give you the opportunity to grow your gifts, increasing the impact and potentially spreading out the legacy for many generations.

A vital part of planning during this career stage is **preparing for retirement**. Just as you divide your spending money according to a budget, it's important to allocate your savings among short-term, long-term and retirement goals.

Fewer than half of households in the 55-64 age group have any retirement savings at all. Although that is an alarming statistic, the best way to avoid being a part of it is to start with a plan. The details are outside the scope of this book, but whether you or your loved ones are close to retirement or many years away, use a trusted adviser to develop a plan and help you stick with it.

The ideal retirement is different for everyone. Many people enjoy what they do and have no desire to quit working. Others are counting down the seconds until they can quit. Some are forced to retire because of their health, a family member's health, inability to find a new job, etc. The worst scenario is being forced to work into old age because you don't have enough money. Since there are so many unknowns, you should not simply drift into this stage of life. It takes years of saving, investing, discipline, delayed gratification and planning to achieve retirement goals.

The best course of action is to start now. The younger you begin, the easier it will be to reach your personal objectives because you have that many more years of compound interest. Paint your ideal picture of retirement, and then work with an advisor and develop a plan to reach that goal. Your dreams can change over time, so adjust your plans accordingly along the way.

If your goal is to work as long as possible because you enjoy what you do, develop a plan to save enough to cover you if an unforeseen circumstance forces you to stop earlier than you would have liked. If you want to retire at 55, travel the world and spend lots of time with your family, you had better get an aggressive savings and investment plan started right away.

Retirement planning heavily relies on the key stewardship principle of delayed gratification, resisting a smaller but more immediate reward in order to receive a larger or more enduring reward later. And the planning doesn't stop once you have retired, as we will see in the next chapter.

9 LIFE STAGE - RETIREMENT

Congratulations! You've arrived at retirement (or else you're peeking at this chapter in hopes for the future). If you have planned well and haven't been hit with unforeseen circumstances like poor health, this life stage should be a reward for a job well done.

When you hear the term "retirement," what do you think? Do you see your house packed with grandkids, volunteering at your church and favorite charities, and traveling to all the places you have always wanted to see? The statistics indicate that those dreams never become a reality for most Americans. Why?

Retirement is a fairly recent concept. In 1935, Social Security was created as a safety net for employees. It established 65 as the normal retirement age, at a time when the average life expectancy was roughly 60 years old. A safe bet for the government!

As time has gone on, medicine, hygiene and other factors have drastically increased Americans' life expectancy, multiplying the number of seniors at the same time that the pool of younger workers who support them is shrinking. This puts the whole system in jeopardy.

Even if it survives in its present form, Social Security was designed to replace roughly thirty percent of a person's income. So, living many years on Social Security alone would likely change one's lifestyle dramatically. The dreams that most people associate with retirement will likely remain dreams, unless they have a Plan B.

The decision to leave the workforce and the comfort of a paycheck can be nerve-racking. You are drawing down a savings that you hope will not go to zero while you are still alive. A **retirement income plan** can help put those nerves at ease, because it gives you control over the inevitable outflow of your precious resources.

The first step is to identify a **trusted advisor**. As Proverbs 24:6 states, "In an abundance of counselors there is victory." A quality advisor will seek to understand your hopes, dreams, goals and financial capabilities, then act as a guide in helping you turn that into a reality. He or she will help you develop a well-thought-out plan, and coach you with a ton of empathy and a dose of tough love through the emotional pitfalls of investing. It takes a guide with an outside perspective to navigate through all of the fads, fears, doubts, worries and misunderstandings that relentlessly attack us all.

The second step is to analyze and evaluate your financial status. This goes far beyond looking at your retirement accounts. It includes, but is not limited to, your tax situation, spending, savings, housing, estate plans, debt and other liabilities.

Once the advisor understands your hopes and has a clear picture of your financial status, he can move to Step Three and begin developing recommendations. These should be in line with your goals, financial capabilities and risk tolerance.

Step Four is communication. The

success of a retirement income plan is based on it being communicated accurately, efficiently and carefully. You may need to go over the plan several times with your advisor to ensure you fully understand and accept it.

Step Five brings us to implementation. Here, you will be responsible for some tasks, and it may even include another professional, such as a CPA or attorney. A spending plan will be part of the implementation process. Changing from a paycheck to a retirement income plan doesn't change the need for a budget. This frees you to know how much money you have coming in every month and where each dollar is going.

The final step of the retirement income plan is monitoring it. Careful monitoring is important, but it is also important not to overdo it. If you find yourself watching the daily movements of your investments, you will likely end up sick or very anxious. Periodic checkups help you avoid the emotional roller coaster. A well-designed retirement income plan will be built for short-term bumps in the road, and sticking to the plan rather than acting emotionally is key. In this ongoing step, your advisor will also monitor changing income needs, health concerns and any other life changes that might occur.

The **cost of healthcare** is one of the main factors the controls many people's retirement decisions. Those who retire prior to age 65 must find healthcare coverage until eligible for Medicare. Some of the possible solutions are: coverage through a spouse's plan, employer-provided retiree coverage, and individual insurance plans. Once you are eligible for Medicare, there are many considerations and additional supplemental options. We will avoid getting into the details, since there are likely to be changes made in the near-term. It is best to consult with an advisor to help make the best possible decision for your particular circumstance.

Long-term care is another major concern for retirees today. Modern medicine, technology and education have helped extend our lives, often into the late 80s and 90s. Nearly 70% of those aged 65 and older will need some kind of extended care, and it can be extremely expensive, leaving family members in a tough spot when it has not been planned for. Purchasing long-term care insurance in your 50s is often the ideal time frame, but that does vary from person to person.

Finally, I'd like to re-emphasize the importance of an **estate plan**. This may seem like something for the rich and famous, but it is much simpler than it sounds. It is really the lifelong process of deciding what to do with your property, which includes houses, cars, investments, jewelry, etc. We talked about a will and a living trust in Chapter 8, and some more thoughts are presented in the next chapter.

Whatever estate plans you make, be sure they are **communicated effectively**. This allows the future beneficiaries to understand the heart behind the gift. Although some plans explicitly dictate where each dollar is to go, most of them pass it on to various places and people for use at their discretion. Not only will early communication put some meaning behind the money, it also provides great opportunities for educating those involved and providing perspective on how the estate came to be. It allows your heirs to carry out the directive in 1 Peter 4:10, "As each has received a gift, use it to serve one another, as good stewards of God's varied grace."

10 YOUR LEGACY

Legendary investor and philanthropist Sir. John Templeton once said, "The best investment with the least risk and greatest dividend is giving." I have yet to meet someone near the end of their life who wishes they had acquired more stuff or made more money. The regrets you consistently hear are that they wish they had spent more time with their loved ones. Their fondest memories are always about giving to and being with others. Although you cannot take anything with you when you go, you can certainly leave a legacy with a multi-generational impact.

What are you planning to leave behind? If you have followed the advice in the preceding chapters, you perhaps have an accumulation of wealth that can be shared with family and causes that are dear to you. This falls under the definition of **philanthropy**, which is "the desire to promote the welfare of others, expressed especially by the generous donation of money to good causes."

With a vast array of worthy causes, it can be very difficult to choose where to allocate your **charitable giving**. Start with prayer. If we believe that God owns it all and we are stewards of what he has entrusted to us, we should look at each dollar or resource and ask, "What would He want me to do with this?" We all play a unique part in his plan and have been uniquely called to give and serve.

Then spend some time with "due diligence." When considering charities, dig deep and find out if they truly match your values and goals. This can help you say no to otherwise worthy causes, perhaps because they spend too much on fundraising. You would hate to give to an organization that is doing some great things, but later find out that they also do some things that do not align with your core beliefs and values.

A good steward will **give strategically**. For example, let's say you wanted to donate

$10,000 to a non-profit organization. You plan to use appreciated stock for this. Assuming the stock was originally purchased for $5,000, if you sell the stock and write a check to the non-profit, the amount would be $9,250 after paying capital gains tax. However, if you were to give the stock directly and have them sell it, they would receive the full $10,000, and you would avoid $750 in capital gains tax. This is a very basic example, but there are many strategies to maximize one's giving potential. A prudent steward looks for ways to increase giving capacity and kingdom impact.

One great philanthropic tool that many people use is a **donor-advised account**. It allows people to fund a charitable account with cash, stocks, real estate, etc., receive an immediate tax benefit, and then allocate grants from the fund to charities of their choice over time. Simplicity, convenience, and even great generosity are a few of the top reasons people establish a donor-advised account.

If you are a person who gives to multiple causes every year, such an account allows you to do this easily, and you only have to manage one receipt for tax-reporting purposes. It also provides you the opportunity to give anonymously, if that is your preference, and to donate strategically. For example, you could put real estate into the account, then take the proceeds and grant them to as many charities as you wish. Or you could keep your gifts invested and growing, allowing you to have a greater impact over time.

And what about the assets you leave behind to your family? How can you help your heirs to value and manage your legacy? There is no right or wrong way to approach **wealth perpetuation**. Some people want to spend or give away every dime by the time they pass away. Others want to leave everything to their children and let them decide how to manage it. Still others leave the entire amount to charity.

Whatever you decide, don't leave wealth perpetuation to chance. Connect the next generation with your advisors to help establish clarity and transparency regarding your financial status and alleviate common fears such as parents running out of money. It's a good idea to have a series of family meetings to discuss the resources they will be entrusted with, or to let them know that your plan is to leave some or all of it to charity. Such discussions may also help them manage their own resources and increase their financial knowledge.

Some points to consider:

- Are your beneficiaries capable of managing the resources you intend to leave them? If not, consider structuring a trust that has guardrails set for them.
- The emotional connection can lead some beneficiaries to make irrational decisions or no decision at all. If you think your beneficiaries will have a difficult time dealing with your passing, consider using a third party trustee to act as a fiduciary in the best interests of your heirs.
- Will a large gift to charity have a long-term impact? Or would a series of smaller gifts be of greater effect? During your lifetime, you have the ability not only to decide who gets what, but also how they receive it. Use your discernment and advisor's counsel to determine the structure that will yield the greatest results.

You worked hard to earn money and probably sacrificed in order to build a legacy. It's important to pursue value for every dime and make sure it's not spent frivolously. Take a warning from the experience of lottery winners. According to a 2012 Vanderbilt University study, 70 percent of them ended up bankrupt.

Additionally, the more money they received, the more likely they were to go broke.

     With proper planning and counsel, you can help insure that your heirs are not like them.

11 CONCLUSION

We approach stewardship through different lenses, based on where we believe God is leading us. This book was written as a tool to help you think about different stewardship ideas, and hopefully expose some areas that you have not yet considered. If you leave this book with a handful of questions, we have accomplished our goal. If you find one or two ideas to use, teach or model, the time invested was worth it.

People's financial histories can be messy. I have wasted plenty of time and money on foolish things that seemed so important at the time. For example, I had a 1999 Range Rover. I probably could have hired a private driver for less money than that car cost me. There are plenty of poor stewardship decisions in my life, leading to a broken picture of my financial past. Remember, "For all have sinned and fall short of the glory of God" (Romans 3:23 NIV). Regardless of your past decisions, each day we are faced with hundreds of new stewardship choices to make.

In the midst of debt, a job loss or other financial hardships, it is easy to feel like broken glass. Sharp, irreparable shards can be scattered all over the place. People who try to help can easily get cut or wounded. But don't despair, no matter what situation you find yourself in.

Many years before the advent of recycling and landfills, trash was dumped into the ocean, including glass. Sharp-edged pieces of glass are slowly refined over many years into beautiful, sought-after treasures. The glass is smoothed and its rough edges softened, while its color and texture are enhanced. It travels with the currents, is tossed by the waves and rubs on the rocks and coarse sand until it has been transformed from broken glass into "sea glass." It washes up on beaches, only to be pulled back out to nature's giant tumbler, until one day it is found and cherished by someone who truly appreciates its rich history, value and beauty.

Like sea glass, our stewardship journeys are long and can be very challenging at times. There will be periods of peace and great joy, and also occasions where we feel as if we are being scraped against the rocks, tossed in the waves and dragged by the changing tides. If we approach each decision with a focus on stewarding resources that are not ours and making a better decision after a failure, we will be refined and made more beautiful day after day.

We are not defined by our past, whether good or bad, yet God can certainly use our past to masterfully grow and shape us. Like sea glass, we are not characterized by our original broken state, although it does play a role in what we have become today. We are defined by the use we have made of our knowledge and experience.

Stewardship is not about how much you have, it is all about what you do with what you have. "Therefore, if anyone is in Christ, the new creation has come: The old has gone, the new is here!" (2 Corinthians 5:17 NIV).

12 STARTING POINTS

At this point you might be feeling overwhelmed. If many of these are new ideas take them one at a time starting with the most impactful. A great place to start if you are overwhelmed is to meet with a financial advisor. They can help you prioritize the appropriate steps to move towards your personal goals and objectives.

Birth to Kindergarten:

- **Establish the foundation:** By personally acknowledging that God owns it all and modeling that your children will start to grasp this foundational principle.
- **Establishing a work ethic:** Again at this stage more is caught than taught. A great place to start for this age group is to encourage them to complete everything they start. For example if they sign up for a sport and decide they don't like it, insist that they finish the season and reevaluate their interest next year.
- **Delayed Gratification:** First, try to resist most impulse buys. This may make it is impossible to take your kids to the store with you without a major meltdown but there is a lot of wisdom in sleeping on a decision to make a purchase, especially large purchases. Delayed gratification can have a significant impact on one's self control and emotional intelligence. Practice it early and often.
    - Try the marshmallow game: Give a child one marshmallow and explain that if they wait 10

minutes to eat that marshmallow they will get another one.

- **Giving:** One of the best ways to help your children and grandchildren learn the joy of giving is by including them in your own giving. Make it a family act.
    - o Talk to them about your own tithing.
    - o Around Christmas you can build an Operation Christmas Child gift box together.
    - o You can make dinner for another family.
    - o You can fundraise for a good cause as a family.
    - o Children can earn money to purchase a gift for another family member or friend.

Elementary School:

- **Allowance:** Start small and give them an expense that they now have to be responsible for. For example, give them an allowance and have them be responsible for their lunch each week. They can decide to budget the allowance to last all week, save the money and pack a lunch, or spend it all and have to figure it out.
- **Limited Resources:** Take a child to the store to spend their money. Let them pick something that cost more than they have. When they get to the checkout counter and they are informed they do not have enough money, walk them back to put it back and talk to them about how much it cost and how much more they will need to save if they really want it.
- **Compare Prices:** Take your kids shopping and have them participate in price comparison. Show them a pair of designer jeans versus a regular pair.
- **Have a Family Finance Meeting:** Sit down as a family and talk about family expenses. You don't need to go into all the details but it provides them perspective on many things they likely take for granted.

High School:

Saving/Investing:

Savings Growth of $100 Deposited Monthly

Depending on the rate of return, depositing just $100 a month into an investment
account and then letting it compound can generate a surprisingly large nest egg

Interest Rate	5 Years	10 Years	15 Years	20 Years	25 Years	30 Years	35 Years	40 Years	Total Invested at 40 Years
$100/mo invested at 2.0%	$6,315	$13,294	$21,006	$29,529	$38,947	$49,355	$60,856	$73,566	$48,000
$100/mo invested at 3.0%	$6,481	$14,009	$22,754	$32,912	$44,712	$58,419	$74,342	$92,837	$48,000
$100/mo invested at 4.0%	$6,652	$14,774	$24,691	$36,800	$51,584	$69,636	$91,678	$118,590	$48,000
$100/mo invested at 5.0%	$6,829	$15,593	$26,840	$41,275	$59,799	$83,573	$114,083	$153,238	$48,000
$100/mo invested at 6.0%	$7,012	$16,470	$29,227	$49,435	$69,646	$100,954	$143,183	$200,145	$48,000
$100/mo invested at 7.0%	$7,201	$17,409	$31,881	$52,397	$81,480	$122,709	$181,156	$264,012	$48,000
$100/mo invested at 8.0%	$7,397	$18,417	$34,835	$59,295	$95,737	$150,030	$230,918	$351,428	$48,000
$100/mo invested at 9.0%	$7,599	$19,497	$38,124	$67,290	$112,953	$184,447	$296,385	$471,643	$48,000
$100/mo invested at 10.0%	$7,808	$20,655	$41,792	$76,570	$133,789	$227,933	$382,828	$637,678	$48,000
$100/mo invested at 11.0%	$8,025	$21,899	$45,886	$87,357	$159,058	$283,023	$497,347	$867,896	$48,000
$100/mo invested at 12.0%	$8,249	$23,234	$50,458	$99,915	$189,764	$352,991	$649,527	$1,188,242	$48,000

Compound Interest:

The Importance of Time and Compounding for the Long Term

The following hypothetical reflects investing $1,200 per year starting at age 20 until retirement at age 65 with an average 11% return. You will also find the approximate amount you would need to invest annually to catch-up with the investor who started at age 20. The column of consequence is the **Total Out-of-Pocket**.

Years until retirement	Annual amount invested	Average annual compound return	Total compounded account value	Total Out-of-pocket	Estimated retirement income
45 years	$1,200.00	11%	$1,445,639.00	**$54,000.00**	$86,738.34
40 years	$2,000.00	11%	$1,421,656.00	**$80,000.00**	$85,299.36
35 years	$3,450.00	11%	$1,441,200.00	**$120,750.00**	$86,472.00
30 years	$5,925.00	11%	$1,444,547.00	**$177,750.00**	$86,672.82
25 years	$10,250.00	11%	$1,440,988.00	**$256,250.00**	$86,459.28
20 years	$18,000.00	11%	$1,427,894.00	**$360,000.00**	$85,673.64
15 years	$33,500.00	11%	$1,439,647.00	**$502,500.00**	$86,378.82
10 years	$67,000.00	11%	$1,433,857.00	**$670,000.00**	$86,031.42
5 years	$168,000.00	11%	$1,444,450.00	**$840,000.00**	$86,667.00

Opportunity Cost: If you are a Starbucks addict of have another daily vice, try for a month to skip that stop and pay yourself the amount you would have spent. At the end of the month, add up the dollars saved and see if you enjoy the $150 +/- in your pocket or prefer the cup of joe. The longer your practice this activity, the great you will feel the opportunity cost.

Year	Starbucks Forgone	Value If Invested
1	$ 1,800.00	$1,980.00
2	$ 3,600.00	$4,158.00
3	$ 5,400.00	$6,553.80
4	$ 7,200.00	$9,189.18
5	$ 9,000.00	$12,088.10
6	$ 10,800.00	$15,276.91
7	$ 12,600.00	$18,784.60
8	$ 14,400.00	$22,643.06
9	$ 16,200.00	$26,887.36
10	$ 18,000.00	$31,556.10
11	$ 19,800.00	$36,691.71
12	$ 21,600.00	$42,340.88
13	$ 23,400.00	$48,554.97
14	$ 25,200.00	$55,390.47
15	$ 27,000.00	$62,909.51
16	$ 28,800.00	$71,180.47
17	$ 30,600.00	$80,278.51
18	$ 32,400.00	$90,286.36
19	$ 34,200.00	$101,295.00
20	$ 36,000.00	$113,404.50
21	$ 37,800.00	$126,724.95
22	$ 39,600.00	$141,377.44
23	$ 41,400.00	$157,495.19
24	$ 43,200.00	$175,224.71
25	$ 45,000.00	$194,727.18
26	$ 46,800.00	$216,179.90
27	$ 48,600.00	$239,777.88
28	$ 50,400.00	$265,735.67
29	$ 52,200.00	$294,289.24
30	$ 54,000.00	$325,698.16
31	$ 55,800.00	$360,247.98
32	$ 57,600.00	$398,252.78
33	$ 59,400.00	$440,058.06
34	$ 61,200.00	$486,043.86
35	$ 63,000.00	$536,628.25
36	$ 64,800.00	$592,271.07
37	$ 66,600.00	$653,478.18
38	$ 68,400.00	$720,806.00
39	$ 70,200.00	$794,866.60
40	$ 72,000.00	$876,333.26

*Chart assumes $1,800/year and an annual return of 10%.

College:

- **The Cost of a College Education:** If you are paying for your child's college education make sure you communicate the cost. You may even want to break down the cost per class so they appreciate the sacrifice that was made for them to be there and avoid the temptation to skip class or take it for granted.
  If student loans are being utilized, make sure your student knows how much they are borrowing and how much they are going to owe upon graduation. It is easy to borrow money when the payments are differed because you don't feel the pain of repayment. Help your student value the privilege they have and maximize the opportunity they have.

- **Internships:** An internship is a great way for a young person to see whether a particular field is of interest or not. Some know what they want to do and find an internship that confirms their desire. It sometimes turns into a job offer, or is at least a great addition to their resume. Others discover that the reality of a particular job doesn't match the dream. Regardless, an internship allows a person to try something, when the stakes are low, and see if it's worth all the effort and education.

- **Tithing:** This is where the rubber meets the road. Tithing while in college, a time when most people have very little income, can take a tremendous leap of faith. Yet what better time to practice the principle in Luke 16:10-12.

Career:

- **Create a Plan:** At this point in life, find a few trusted advisors to help you create a plan. Take inventory of where you are at and then paint the picture of where you would like to be. A financial advisor can help you develop a plan to reach all of your dreams and also establish some priorities.

Retirement:

- **Retirement Income Plan:** Retirement is the point where you trade your employment paycheck for distributions from your retirement savings and investments. It is crucial that you sit down with an advisor to develop your individual plan so you can enter this phase with confidence. Guessing at this stage of the game can be devastating. A plan gives you the freedom to confidently walk through retirement knowing how your decisions will impact your financial future.

Legacy:

- **Give Strategically:** Check with your advisor to determine the best ways to give. A few simple techniques can greatly increase your impact.

- **Wisdom & Discernment:** Seek God's will on a daily basis but also ask God to show you what to do with all that he has trusted you with after death. Although you cannot take anything with you when you go, you can certainly leave a legacy with a multi-generational impact.

13 BIBLICAL PERSPECTIVES
Eight Financial Principles from the Bible

1. **Work Hard** – Work as for the Lord. God gave us the ability to work, so avoid the temptation of being lazy. "For even when we were with you, we gave you this rule: The one who is unwilling to work shall not eat" (2 Thessalonians 3:10 NIV).

2. **Earn Money** – It is not wrong to earn money. "Anyone who does not provide for their relatives, and especially for their own household, has denied the faith and is worse than an unbeliever" (1 Timothy 5:8 NIV).

3. **Give a Tithe Back to God First** – Tithing (10% of income) acknowledges that it is God's money and you are a steward over what he has entrusted to you. A tithe is an act of trusting that God will provide. ""Bring the whole

tithe into the storehouse, that there may be food in my house. Test me in this,' says the LORD Almighty, 'and see if I will not throw open the floodgates of heaven and pour out so much blessing that there will not be room enough to store it'" (Malachi 3:10 NIV).

4. **Save** – It is wise to save a portion of your earnings for future expenses. "A good person leaves an inheritance for their children's children, but a sinner's wealth is stored up for the righteous" (Proverbs 13:22 NIV).

5. **Avoid Debt** – When you are in debt to someone, you have an obligation to them. As much as possible you should remain obligated to God only. "The rich rule over the poor, and the borrower is slave to the lender" (Proverbs 22:7 NIV).

6. **Be Generous** – God calls us to build his Kingdom with the money he entrusts to us. There is much joy in giving when God leads you to give. "Each of you should give what you have decided in your heart to give, not reluctantly or under compulsion, for God loves a cheerful giver" (2 Corinthians 9:7 NIV).

7. **Be Content** – The love of money and possessions can take over your life and ruin it. "For where your treasure is, there your heart will be also" (Matthew 6:21 NIV).

8. **Don't Let Money Become Your Master** – God is your master. Money should only be a tool to glorify God. "No one can serve two masters. Either you will hate the one and love the other, or you will be devoted to the one and despise the other. You cannot serve both God and money" (Matthew 6:24 NIV).

14 FINANCIAL TERMS

Asset – Any item you own (e.g. house, investments, car) that can be converted into cash, as well as any money that is owed to you.

Beneficiary – A person who is named on your life insurance policies or retirement plans to receive the benefit after you die.

Bond – An investment in which one loans money to a corporation or government entity and earns interest on that debt until it is repaid at a predetermined time.

Cash flow – Money you have coming in (e.g. salary) and money you have going out (e.g. mortgage payments). Positive cash flow means you have more coming in than going out. Negative cash flow means you are spending more than you earn.

Collateral – Assets you pledge to secure a loan or credit which can be taken by the lender after a period of time if you default on the payments (e.g. a line of credit on your home).

Compound interest – Interest that is calculated on the principal loan amount as well as on any interest that has already accrued. This makes your investments grow faster and is a key benefit of investing at an early age.

Credit rating – An evaluation of your ability and likelihood to make payments or default on a loan or credit.

Credit score – A number based on your credit rating that lenders can use to decide if they will lend you money, how much they will lend you and the interest you will pay on the loan.

Diversification – A technique that reduces risk by allocating investments among various financial instruments, industries, and other categories. It aims to maximize return by investing in different areas that would each react differently to the same event.

Dividend – A distribution of a portion of a company's earnings, paid to a class of its shareholders.

Dollar-Cost Averaging (DCA) – An investment technique of buying a fixed dollar amount of a particular investment on a regular schedule, regardless of the share price. The investor purchases more shares when prices are low and fewer shares when prices are high.

Estate planning – The process of planning what will happen with your assets after you die. Wills, investment products and life insurance policies are part of your estate plan.

ETF (Exchange Traded Fund) – An investment that is similar to a mutual fund, but trades like a stock on an exchange, experiencing price changes throughout the day. ETFs tend to be cheaper than mutual funds in terms of fees, because they aren't managed by a person but instead are designed to move up or down along with the market for certain types of commodities or companies.

Investments – Investments include financial products, real estate or other assets which may grow in value, which you put money into in order to help reach your financial goals.

Inflation – The rate at which the average prices for goods and services rise each year, which lowers the purchasing power of your dollar. For example, if inflation is at 2%, you will be able to buy 2% less next year with the same amount of money.

Liabilities – Funds that you owe such as a mortgage, other loans or taxes as well as any interest on them.

Liquidity – The ability to quickly convert assets to cash. Cash is purely liquid but investments or real estate are less liquid because they need to be sold before money is obtained.

Matching contribution – Money your employer adds to your retirement savings account, such as a 401(k) based on a percentage of the money you have put into it.

Mutual Fund – An investment made up of a collection of stocks, bonds or other investments. Buying a mutual fund enables the investor to easily diversify without buying a number of investments. Mutual funds are run by money managers, who invest according to the stated investment objectives of the fund.

Permanent life insurance – Life insurance that does not expire and is designed to be in place for the rest of your life.

Risk tolerance – The degree of variability in investment returns that an investor is willing to withstand.

Stock – Also known as a "share" or "equity," a stock is a type of investment vehicle that gives the stockholder part ownership of a corporation and a claim on part of its assets and earnings.

Term life insurance – Life insurance that is in place for a specific term (e.g. 10 years) and is designed to pay a benefit if you die during the term.

Underwriting – The process an insurance company goes through to decide whether or not to insure you, set the premium and issue a policy. This is usually based on a variety of factors including your age, health and lifestyle.

Yield – The income return on an investment, such as the interest or dividends received from holding a particular security.

REFERENCES

(1) Cornfield, J. (2017, January 12). *Bankrate.com.* Retrieved from https://www.bankrate.com/finance/consumer-index/money-pulse-0117.aspx

(2) Hellmich, N. (2014, August 18). *A third of People have nothing saved for retirment.* Retrieved from USA Today: https://www.usatoday.com/story/money/personal finance/2014/08/18/zero-retirement-savings/14070167/

(3) Kador, J. (2015, March). Love and Marriage. *REP. Wealth Management* .

(4) Crown. (2015, July 1). *Money & Possession Scriptures.* Retrieved from Crown.org: http://www.crown.org/wp-content/uploads/2017/05/2300ScriptureReferences-7.1.15.pdf

(5) Wilson, R. (2017, April 3). *Census: More Americans have college degrees than ever before.* Retrieved from The Hill: http://thehill.com/homenews/state-watch/326995-census-more-americans-have-college-degrees-than-ever-before

ABOUT THE AUTHOR

Rob is an investment adviser at J. Derek Lewis & Associates in Newport Beach, where he also serves as the Chief Executive Officer. JDL exist to guide individuals in their stewardship responsibilities over the resources with which they have been blessed. Rob is the husband to his high school sweetheart Holly and the father to three amazing children, Brady, Brock, & Sadie. Rob is on a crusade helping others get a hold of their finances and walk confidently in their stewardship responsibilities.

CONTACT INFORMATION

If this book has left you with unanswered questions or has helped you in any way, I would love to hear from you.

Email: Rob@JDLA-Adviers.com
Websites: www.JDLA-Advisers.com
www.robknutsen.me
Instagram: @stewardfromthestart

45332795R00058

Made in the USA
San Bernardino, CA
28 July 2019